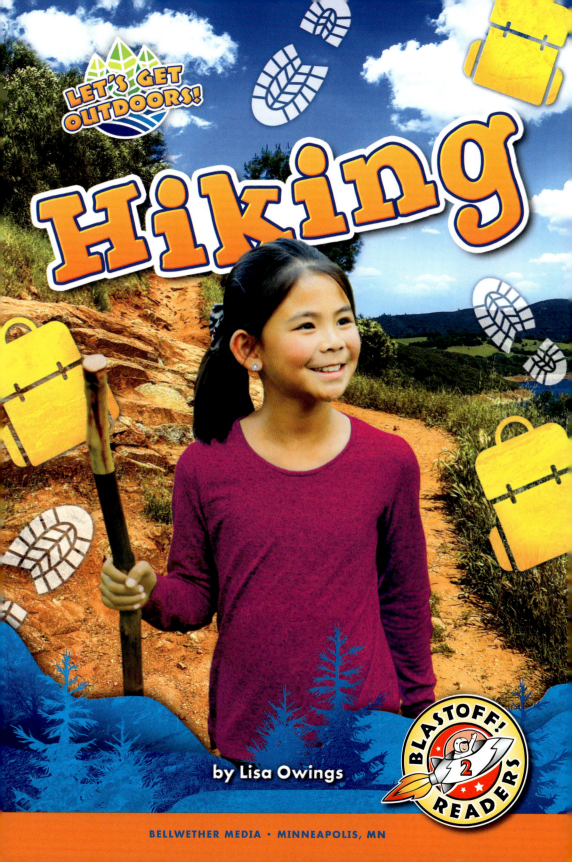

Blastoff! Readers are carefully developed by literacy experts to build reading stamina and move students toward fluency by combining standards-based content with developmentally appropriate text.

 Level 1 provides the most support through repetition of high-frequency words, light text, predictable sentence patterns, and strong visual support.

 Level 2 offers early readers a bit more challenge through varied sentences, increased text load, and text-supportive special features.

 Level 3 advances early-fluent readers toward fluency through increased text load, less reliance on photos, advancing concepts, longer sentences, and more complex special features.

★ **Blastoff! Universe**

Reading Level

 Grade K 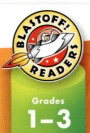 Grades 1–3  Grade 4

This edition first published in 2023 by Bellwether Media, Inc.

No part of this publication may be reproduced in whole or in part without written permission of the publisher. For information regarding permission, write to Bellwether Media, Inc., Attention: Permissions Department, 6012 Blue Circle Drive, Minnetonka, MN 55343.

Library of Congress Cataloging-in-Publication Data

LC record for Hiking available at: https://lccn.loc.gov/2022038741

Text copyright © 2023 by Bellwether Media, Inc. BLASTOFF! READERS and associated logos are trademarks and/or registered trademarks of Bellwether Media, Inc.

Editor: Rebecca Sabelko   Series Design: Andrea Schneider   Book Designer: Laura Sowers

Printed in the United States of America, North Mankato, MN.

Table of Contents

What Is Hiking?	4
Take a Hike!	8
Hiking Gear	14
Hiking Safety	18
Glossary	22
To Learn More	23
Index	24

What Is Hiking?

Hiking is taking a walk in nature!

Many people hike to enjoy the world's beauty on foot. It is also a way to exercise.

Parks and forests are common hiking spots. Hikers can take short walks on trails.

Favorite Hiking Spot

The Appalachian Trail

Claim to Fame

- runs nearly 2,200 miles (3,541 kilometers) through 14 states

- longest hiking-only footpath in the world

trekking a mountain

They can also **trek** up mountains. Hikers explore different landscapes!

Take a Hike!

Hikers choose a **route** to follow. It is best to start with easy hikes.

Hikers can work up to longer, steeper routes.

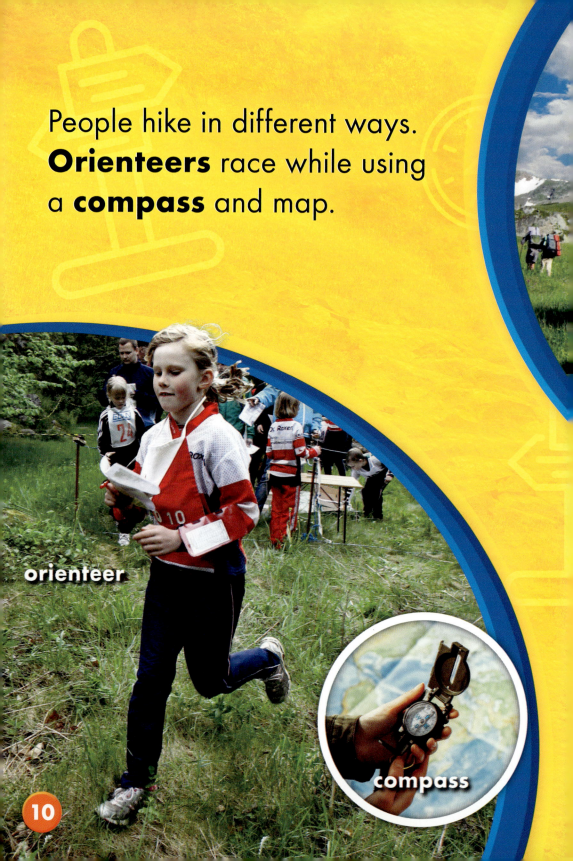

People hike in different ways. **Orienteers** race while using a **compass** and map.

orienteer

compass

Mountaineers hike up mountain trails. **Backpackers** hike between camps each night.

Most people find trails close to home. Others plan hiking trips across countries.

The best kind of hike is one the hiker enjoys!

Trail Signs

straight

right turn

left turn

trail start

trail end

new trail

Hiking Gear

Hikers must wear shoes or boots that fit well. They must also dress for the weather.

A map, compass, or **GPS** keeps hikers from getting lost.

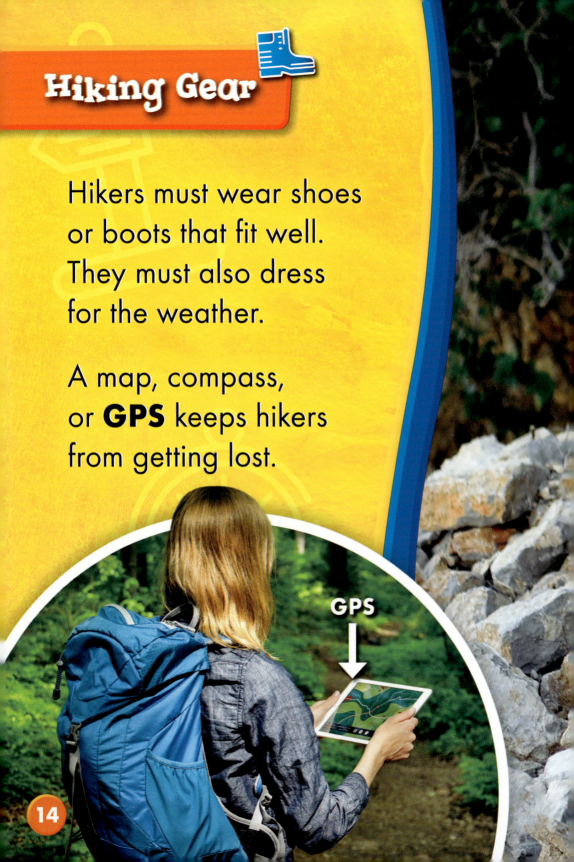

GPS

hiking shoes

Hikers must carry enough food and water for their hike. Backpackers need camping gear.

Hiking Gear

- compass
- water
- shoes
- first-aid kit

first-aid kit

Emergency tools include matches and a **first-aid kit**.

Hiking Safety

It is always safest to hike with others. Hikers stay on marked trails.

They also stay away from wild animals and dangerous areas.

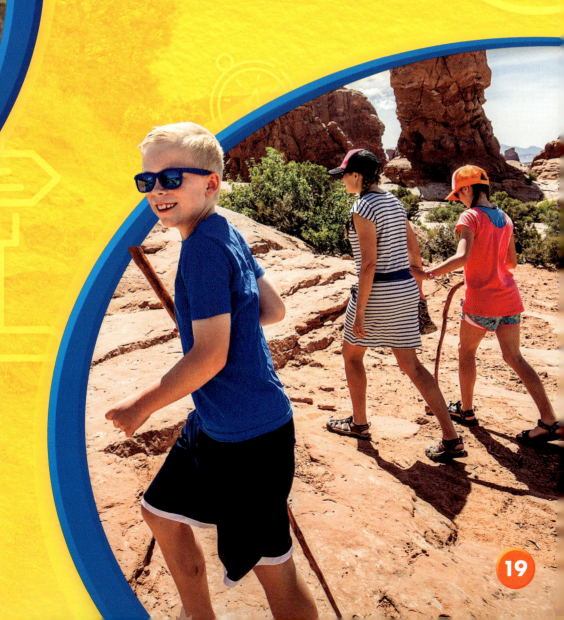

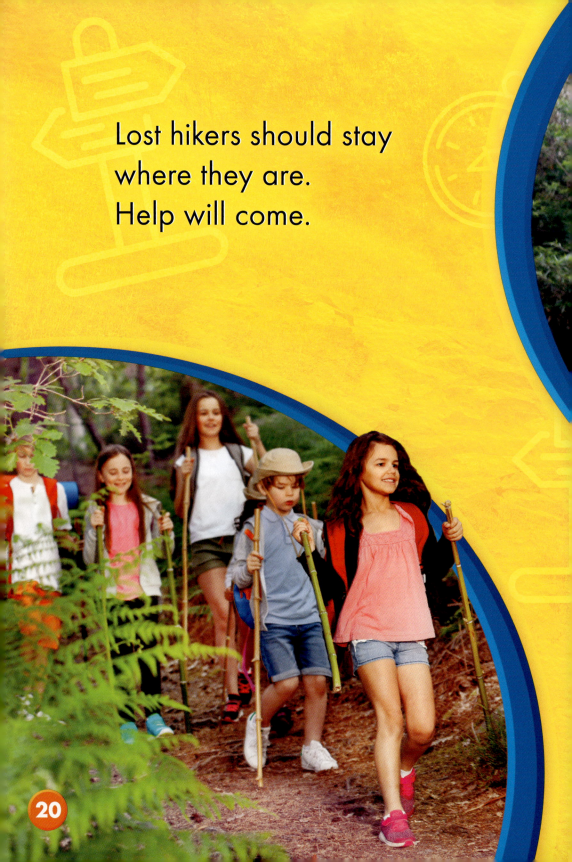

Lost hikers should stay where they are. Help will come.

Hikers look down to avoid falling. But they look up to enjoy nature's beauty!

Glossary

backpackers—hikers who carry all their camping gear in backpacks; backpackers often camp at a different site each night.

compass—a tool that shows direction; compasses have a magnetic needle that points north.

emergency—related to a sudden need for help or relief

first-aid kit—an emergency set of supplies for treating a sick or injured person

GPS—global positioning system; GPS is a system people use to find locations.

mountaineers—people who hike up mountains for sport

orienteers—hikers who compete in a timed race using a map and compass to find their way on a trail

route—a course of travel

trek—to travel through a difficult landscape

To Learn More

AT THE LIBRARY

Oswald, Pete. *Hike*. Somerville, Mass.: Candlewick Press, 2020.

Sumerak, Marc. *Survival Handbook: An Essential Companion to the Great Outdoors.* Bellevue, Wash.: Becker&Mayer! kids, 2019.

Thermes, Jennifer. *Grandma Gatewood Hikes the Appalachian Trail.* New York, N.Y.: Abrams Books for Young Readers, 2018.

ON THE WEB

FACTSURFER

Factsurfer.com gives you a safe, fun way to find more information.

1. Go to www.factsurfer.com.

2. Enter "hiking" into the search box and click 🔍.

3. Select your book cover to see a list of related content.

Index

animals, 19
backpackers, 11, 16
boots, 14
camps, 11, 16
compass, 10, 14
emergency tools, 17
exercise, 5
favorite spot, 6
first-aid kit, 17
food, 16
forests, 6
gear, 16
GPS, 14
hikers, 6, 7, 8, 13, 14, 16, 18, 20, 21
hikes, 8, 13, 16
map, 10, 14
matches, 17
mountaineers, 11
mountains, 7, 11

nature, 4, 21
orienteers, 10
parks, 6
route, 8
safety, 18, 19, 20, 21
shoes, 14, 15
trail signs, 13
trails, 6, 11, 12, 18
trek, 7
trips, 12
walk, 4, 6
water, 16

The images in this book are reproduced through the courtesy of: FatCamera/ Getty Images, front cover; Lisa Parsons, front cover (background); New Africa, p. 3; Monkey Business Images, pp. 4-5; vgajic, p. 5; Jonathan A Mauer, p. 6; Maria Sbytova, pp. 6-7, 14-15; Julia Kuznetsova, p. 7; PeopleImages, p. 8; Pat Tr, pp. 8-9; Jeppe Gustafsson/ Alamy, p. 10 (orienteer); Duet PandG, p. 10 (compass); Golden Pixels LLC, pp. 12-13; Petair, p. 14; Dudarev Mikhail, p. 16 (hiker); gd_project, p. 16 (compass); APN Photography, p. 16 (water); javierDan, p. 16 (first-aid kit); karamysh, p. 16 (background); Fertnig, pp. 16-17; SolStock, pp. 18-19; Brocreative, p. 19; Sergey Novikov, p. 20; Siam Stock, pp. 20-21; Max Topchii, p. 22.